The Science, Art and Voodoo of Freelance Pricing and Getting Paid

JAKE POINIER

JAN –
All the best for creating
more passive and active
income for your biz!
JAKE

The Science, Art and Voodoo of Freelance Pricing and Getting Paid

Published by More Cowbell Books, LLC.

Available from Amazon.com, CreateSpace.com, and other retail outlets.

ISBN-13: 978-0615872254
ISBN-10: 0615872255

Book design by Jane Gerke

This publication has been compiled based on personal experience, research, and the author's opinion, but it is not intended to replace legal, financial or other professional advice or services. Every reasonable attempt has been made to provide accurate content, and the author and publisher disclaim responsibility for any errors or omissions contained herein. The samples provided are for educational and discussion purposes only. All website addresses cited were current at the time of publication. Any trademarks, service marks, product names or named features are assumed to be the property of their respective owners and are used solely for editorial reference, not endorsement. And, of course, it's your responsibility to tailor the content to your own business model, experience level, clients, projects, market, religious affiliation, political leanings, weather conditions and other factors.

Or, as they say in the car biz, "Your mileage may vary."

Well, that's more than enough fine print for today. Let's get on to the good stuff!

To everyone who's made

the freelance leap,

and to all the great clients

who've made it possible.

Table of Contents

AN INTRODUCTION
The Science, Art and Voodoo of Freelance Pricing

For our 10th wedding anniversary, my wife and I took a trip to Ecuador. Among many memories, the one that sticks out was a hike through the Amazonian jungle. Outfitted in ancient, knee-high rubber boots, our group slogged through mud, downpours, thick brush and more mud. We saw flocks of parrots, marveled at some of the largest trees I'd ever seen and ate cacao beans right off the plant. At one point on the trail, we got passed as if we'd been standing still by a tiny Ecuadoran woman who held a baby on one hip and a two-foot-long machete on the other.

Several hours later, when the guide announced, "It won't be much longer," we sighed with relief—for a moment. Around the next bend, we saw that the end of our eight-mile trek would be punctuated by traversing a bark-free, rain-soaked, 40-foot log that spanned a mud-filled canyon about 15 feet below us. The fact that the guide nimbly sprinted across offered no solace. The rest of us, painfully aware of the lack of tread and the surplus of jungle mud on our ill-fitting boots, inched over the slick surface.

It wasn't the most dangerous or scariest thing I've ever done, but I'd argue that it illustrates the evolution you make as a freelancer. You can make a hard-fought trek only to find that you've got one more obstacle and are operating without a safety net. Yet, as you gain experience and confidence, those long, slippery logs just aren't as daunting as they once were.

You might guess where I'm going with this analogy: Pricing, estimating, negotiating, collecting and all of the monetary aspects of freelancing can be downright terrifying, but they don't have to be. At first, you might be inching across; once you've got some miles on your boots, you'll be as sure-footed as a native guide.

✷✷✷

Now, let's bring matters out of the jungle and into the marketplace. If I asked you to tell me the current price of a gallon of gas or milk, you'd probably guess within 25 cents, maybe closer. You might be within $50 or $100 of the price of a new computer or flat-screen TV that you're coveting.

But if I ask you the price of a major home improvement project— say, having a new roof put on, a deck built or your kitchen remodeled— you'd likely be hard pressed to estimate the cost within a couple thousand dollars. Moreover, if you asked for bids from three different contractors, they might vary by even more than you guessed.

Three factors are at work here. First is that the gas, milk and home electronics examples feature commodities: items you can get anywhere from the local mall or corner store. Second is that the construction project is a much bigger job involving a lot more X factors. Third, and most important, is that the first few items have almost nothing to do with how much *time* it'll take, whereas that's generally 50% or more of the home improvement cost.

In building, you'll hear the expression "time and materials" as a way of pricing something. (And there's always a staff person whose one and only job is to estimate and price jobs.)

In freelancing, however, the "materials" part of the equation essentially disappears beyond a fraction of your home office, computer and communications costs—and you're on your own to figure out the rest.

The truth is, you can price your creative skills in dozens of ways. None of them is wrong, though some are more profitable than others. Although I focus on examples of writing and editing in this volume, the same rate-setting principles apply to freelancers of all stripes, whether they're graphic/web designers, photographers, public relations pros or illustrators.

In my experience, the process starts with science: What are the empirical, objective facts that warrant a given fee and generate an appropriate profit margin? Then, to implement your rates, you need to incorporate the arts of sales and negotiation: What are the most persuasive methods to secure a signed agreement—and a check once the job is completed? And, finally, there's always a little bit of voodoo, though I'm not suggesting you hand-craft a doll resembling a client from hell and jab it with pins. Think of it in terms of your mindset: What are the unseen aspects of individual projects and your overall business? How can you influence a client relationship or freelance job in a positive direction, even when it starts to go awry?

This book will help you accomplish this process as quickly and as logically as possible: figuring out what your time is worth and then presenting your prices and proposals in the most effective, attractive way to potential clients and turning them into loyal ones.

Jake Poinier
September 2013

📖 **10% of this book's net profits** will be donated to United Through Reading® (UnitedThroughReading.org), a nonprofit organization that helps ease the stress of separation for military families by having deployed parents read children's books aloud via DVD for their child to watch at home.

CHAPTER 1

Engaging Your Business Brain

While it's appealing to think, "Gee, wouldn't it be nice if all I had to do was the creative stuff," getting better at the business end of freelancing will provide you with access to more interesting—and, ultimately, more lucrative—freelance projects. That's your incentive!

Acknowledging and having some pride in your business-oriented alter ego relies on the same principle you use when you force a smile to make yourself happier, or when you stand up straighter to feel more powerful. After all, your creative talents are helping others succeed in their business, right? That's a reason to hold your head high.

Of course, most of us need to make the connection between creativity and money. That seems easy if you Google "earn a six-figure income" or "make millions in your pajamas" only to learn that the world offers many career choices that seemingly guarantee an effortless, leisurely ticket to riches while you work from home. Naturally, freelance writing figures heavily among them.

At the risk of sounding holier-than-thou, I'd say that there are few reasons *worse* to choose an industry than it seems an easy way to skate to $100,000. That's as true of freelancing as it is of anything else. As a part-time rowing coach, I'd rank it every bit as wrongheaded as parents who want their kids to row so they can get into an Ivy League university. Sure, it might work, but is it the right reason to take part in that activity?

Can you earn six figures as a freelancer? Yes, you can. Is becoming a freelancer a great career move? Perhaps. But going in, you should be aware that the market will test your entrepreneurial skills far more than it will ever value your ability to mash a keyboard.

For writers, editors, graphic designers and other creative freelancers, that means engaging your business brain. More specifically, it requires understanding the business processes that will help make you not just successful but an outperformer among your peers, who lament, "*Why can't I just write/edit/proofread/design?*"

But more important, becoming a freelancer requires understanding the root of the issue. It's common advice that you have to monetize your blog or social media efforts. I'm here to tell you that you need to monetize your brain. That includes your hard-fought education, your myriad experiences in business and elsewhere, and, of course, your creative talents. It's taking the sum of everything that's brought you to this point in your career and getting someone to pay you for it. Scary, maybe. But exciting, definitely!

On writing websites, you'll often see a quote from famed screen-writer and essayist Robert Benchley: "The freelance writer is a man who is paid per piece or per word or perhaps." As a writer, he was known for his clever wordplay, but let's just say Benchley's business plan could have used a bit more of a strategic approach—and, heck, maybe even a pep talk to shore up his self-esteem. In the following pages, that's precisely what I strive to provide.

✳ Quick Tip: Embrace Your Inner Salesperson

Most of us aren't natural-born salespeople—and for many of us, selling something, especially our own talents, is downright terrifying. One of the specific steps I always recommend for freelancers is taking seminars in sales techniques and negotiating, particularly if you've never had a corporate job that taught/demanded those skills. You'll find it helps your confidence, and you'll discover that it's not rocket science. It doesn't have to be a session specific to your creative field, and it's probably better that it's not—you're looking to gain a better understanding of the principles, which are universal.

CHAPTER 2

The Unified Theory of Freelance Pricing

The famed artist Pablo Picasso was sipping an espresso at a Paris café when a beautiful woman approached. Boldly, she asked him to do a sketch of her.

Nodding, but without uttering a word, Picasso broke out his pencils and a piece of canvas and set to work. Within a few minutes, he'd created a portrait and handed it to her.

She was shocked at how wonderfully he'd captured her essence in just mere moments.

"Monsieur Picasso, this is lovely," she said. "How much do I owe you?"

"Five thousand dollars," he replied.

"But, why?" she said, now even more shocked at the price tag. "It took you only a few minutes!"

"Mais non, Madame," he said, unswayed by her reaction. "It took a lifetime."

Artistic legends and apocryphal stories aside, my experience is that creatives in general (and freelancers in particular) tend to shoot too low when it comes to pricing—whether it's due to lack of experience or confidence, poor business sense or sales panache, or simply undercharging for doing something they enjoy. Obviously, it's difficult to put a monetary figure on something you've produced through nothing other than the tips of your fingers and the gray matter between your ears.

Both novice freelancers and battle-hardened veterans ask these common questions: "Am I pricing my services correctly?" and "How much should I charge for this job?" While there are no quick solutions—despite the pricing sheets scattered across the internet—a three-component process yields a logical, scientific reason for pricing yourself the way you choose to.

Component #1: Bottom-up Calculation

The first step in developing a pricing scheme for your services is to consider what you need to live on as well as what you want to save from your profits. This is the bottom-up calculation. You can use it whether you're full time or part time; the goal is to figure out your hourly rate, regardless of how many hours that might be.

Pencils ready? Time to roughly assess your current annual expenses. (These don't have to be down to the penny. Ballpark figures will do.)

ANNUAL EXPENSES

General – Living/Household
Mortgage/Rent   _____

Utilities   _____

Groceries   _____

Car/Transportation   _____

Education   _____

Healthcare   _____

Life Insurance   _____

Other   _____

Business Expenses
Computer and Other Equipment   _____

Communications (Phone/Cell, Internet)   _____

Office Supplies   _____

Memberships   _____

Other   _____

Federal Taxes   _____

State/Local Taxes   _____

Fun Stuff
Vacations   _____

Entertainment   _____

Other   _____

Savings/Retirement Plan   _____

Emergency Fund   _____

Miscellaneous   _____

TOTAL ANNUAL EXPENSES $_____

Now, perform some down-and-dirty math with that total. For the purposes of this next equation, you can generally assume about 235 working days per year, which takes into account 104 weekend days, 2 weeks' vacation, 10 legal holidays and 6 sick days. (Note: Even if you're just freelancing on the side, do the calculation as if you're full time for the purposes of this exercise.)

$$\underline{\$\quad\quad\quad\quad} \div \underline{\quad\quad 235 \quad\quad} = \underline{\$\quad\quad\quad\quad}$$

Total expenses ÷ working days/yr. = per-day goal

That's how much you'd need to make per day in order to cover your annual expenditures, working full-time freelance. (See that line about "savings/retirement plan"? Unless you're independently wealthy, make sure you're generous, on the order of 15-20% of your annual income.)

✳ Quick Tip: Do the Math Online

For convenience, use the calculators provided at MoreCowbellBooks.com.

The next step is to consider how many hours per day you believe are billable. Keep in mind, most freelancers may work 8-hour days, but only a fraction of that time is billable. The rest is spent on administration, marketing, networking, blogging and other non-paying tasks. (In my own experience, billable hours account for about 40-60% of my day, though that can vary tremendously.)

$$\underline{\$\quad\quad\quad\quad} \div \underline{\quad\quad\quad\quad} = \underline{\$\quad\quad\quad\quad}$$

Per-day goal ÷ Billable hrs./day = Estimated hourly rate

The resulting number is—you guessed it—the hourly rate you'd need to charge to cover your average annual expenditures and to put some money aside.

Component #2: Top-down Calculation

This calculation is a lot simpler and less time consuming. It means asking, "What do I *want* to earn this year?" If you're coming fresh to a freelance career from a well-paying corporate job, it may not be realistic to match that salary your first year out, but it's certainly reasonable in your sophomore or junior campaign.

The key here is to shoot high, since you are now responsible for health insurance, life insurance, time off, both sides of your Social Security payments and other items that your previous employer was covering for you. According to the most recent Bureau of Labor Statistics data, the average employee benefits package is worth about 30% of the total compensation package. Depending on your personal circumstance, that could mean adding 30% to what your salary was—in other words, a $60,000-a-year job would warrant a $78,000 income goal for this calculation.

So, in an ideal world, what would make you happy and profitable—and not just feeling as if you're living check to check? Again, if you're full time, that's 235 days per year, subtracting weekends, holidays, vacation and a little bit of sick time. Conversely, if you expect to part-time freelance one day a week, just plug in 52.

_____		_____		_____
Income goal	÷	Working days/yr.	=	Goal income/day

That's how much you need to earn per day to meet your goal. As above, now we need to divide this number by a reasonable expectation of billable hours in an average workday.

_____		_____		_____
Goal income/day	÷	Billable hrs./day	=	Estimated hourly rate

Using the top-down calculation, that's the hourly rate you'd need to charge, based on that number of billable hours, to reach that income goal at the end of the year.

Component #3: Market-Based Double-Check

The rate surveys published in *Writer's Market*, the Editorial Freelancers Association and elsewhere on the web aren't a panacea when it comes to setting your hourly rate. The ranges are wide, and there's no way of knowing for sure what your own market will bear; in addition, your rate may be different for a local market than it is for a big-city client. If a source is saying that a writer in your area of expertise is getting $0.10-$2 a word, there's a lot of room for variability based on how many words you can write an hour—not to mention how much work you can acquire at a given rate.

Nonetheless, in conjunction with your calculations above, you can still use these rate sheets to double-check your math from the first two exercises. The categories are broken down sufficiently whether you're a corporate writer, copyeditor, indexer, non-fiction ghostwriter or any other kind of wordsmith. Again, however, they don't take into account your speed, level of experience or target audience.

Finally, using these resources about freelance rates can help you do your own legwork to see what's appropriate in your market. A quick conversation with any or all of the following should do the trick:

- Veteran freelancers
- Graphic designers
- Web designers
- Marketing specialists
- Ad agencies
- Business owners
- Local or LinkedIn freelance groups

Now, keep in mind that many folks will want to keep this information close to the vest. An experienced freelancer might consider it a trade secret; a client might not want to reveal what she pays, thinking she might be able to negotiate a better price. But asking a third party you know—one whom you aren't asking for work—can generally be a good guide.

✳ Quick Tip: As a Daily Reminder
Write your annual and daily income goals on a yellow sticky note and post it on your computer.

Bringing It All Together

You've now developed at least three different perspectives on what your hourly rate should be, give or take a few bucks. If your bottom-up and top-down numbers are close to each other, you may not even need to put much research time into a third-party perspective; your own "personal market" has spoken. If the numbers don't match up, you can gain peace of mind by checking with people who provide or purchase freelance services.

At some point, however, you just need to dive in, knowing that, unlike a retail store, you have the good fortune to be able to change your price for every single transaction. Moreover, you're not simply going to charge by the hour, even though this calculation plays a role in formulating a quote for a client. Which brings us to the subject of our next chapter: the basic principles of estimating.

$$ Pricing Resources

RATE SURVEYS
- *Writer's Market* (WritersMarket.com) publishes print and web versions of an annual "How Much Should I Charge?" feature.
- Editorial Freelancers Association (the-efa.org) does an annual membership survey with about a dozen different rate categories.

RATE CALCULATORS
In addition to what you'll find on MoreCowbellBooks.com, the rate calculators at these websites offer different ways to experiment with your scenarios:

- AllFreelanceWriting.com
- FreelanceSwitch.com

🖳 Should I Post Rates on My Website?

Ah, the subject of never-ending debate on countless freelance websites—and for which there's no definitive answer. If you decide to publish your rates, go with a price range for given services. Doing so is always safer and gives you better negotiating room than naming a single set price or announcing your hourly rate to the world.

That said, here's a quick list of pros and cons to consider:

👍 PROS OF PUBLISHING YOUR RATES
- People know exactly what to expect.
- You'll attract clients who can afford you.
- You'll repel clients who can't afford you.
- You don't have to revisit "What do I charge for that?" all the time.
- You can update your prices quickly.

👎 CONS OF PUBLISHING YOUR RATES
- You might scare away good prospects if prices are too high or if they don't understand your structure.
- You may attract low-ballers if prices are too low.
- Pricing depends on circumstance, so it's tough to make a one-size-fits-all price list.
- You've squandered negotiating leverage if you haven't made the upper range high enough.

CHAPTER 3

The Basic Principles of Estimating

In the previous chapter, we drilled down on what your approximate hourly rate should be. Now it's time to put those figures into action.

But before we crank up the ol' bid machine and throw numbers out to clients and prospects, let's talk a bit about the foundation of sound estimating:

- If you fail to price your skills right, your clients will surely fail to value them properly.
- You can always come down in price once you have presented a bid. You can't go up, unless a client requests additional services.
- Rather than deterring a buying decision, higher rates can imply greater value to a client or prospect.
- If every estimate you send out is accepted without a flinch, you're likely not charging enough.
- If every estimate you send out is rejected, it's not necessarily the price that's killing the deal.
- Being specific about the details is far superior to being open-ended, for both parties.
- Taking a project at a lower rate has what economists call an "opportunity cost": You're not available to solicit or accept better-paying work.
- If you provide exceptional value for your clients, they'll happily refer new business to you.

The challenge, of course, is that there is a huge amount of variability between project types and clients; bidding on a whitepaper is different from developing website content, and copyediting a novel is distinct from ghostwriting a non-fiction business book. Once you accept those differences, you still come back to one of the core principles of this book:

You are monetizing your brain, and you must determine how to use that brain, for how long and for what purpose.

Naturally, estimating is more challenging early in your freelance career, before you have a frame of reference. The good news is that each project gives you a better understanding of your own speed and skills—as well as an ability to read between the lines when clients describe what they want.

Two categories—incorporating various elements of science, art and voodoo—will help you come up with a reasonable estimate.

Category 1 (Science): The Hard Facts

You're sitting down with that blank page staring back at you. Start by asking yourself these key questions about the scope of the project in objective terms. Then, assign an approximate number of hours to each. So, the science portion includes the following:

• **What's the length/format/content I am dealing with, and what am I expected to do to it?** Some examples: Writing 10 web pages with an average of 300 words per page. Heavy editing of 200 pages of a novel with 250 words per page. Scriptwriting for a 5-minute video, at approximately 170 words per minute. Copywriting an 8.5"x 11" bi-fold brochure with about 600 words of text, and supplying 15-20 possible tagline concepts.

• **What materials will be supplied to me vs. original content I am expected to produce?** Interviews and research are time intensive, and you need to assess approximately how much time they will consume—and don't forget how long it takes to transcribe recorded conversations. It will also take you longer, sometimes significantly so, if you are responsible for finding and scheduling the interviewees.

• **How much communications/meeting time does the client expect? Will travel and onsite meetings be involved?** These specific questions are highly individual to each client. Some will want one onsite meeting and weekly or even daily meetings/updates; others require only a startup phone conversation and then a finished product. In case you're wondering: Yes, communications, meetings and travel time should be charged at your standard rate, not a discounted one!

• **Do you need to handle any project or physical tasks unrelated to writing/editing?** Don't overlook the time required for tasks such as uploading files to a content management system/blog/social media outlet, managing an editorial calendar or securing images and signoffs from people you interview.

• **What are the expectations as far as revisions?** Some freelancers will define a specific number of revisions within a contract or agreement, particularly for a new client; others will "write till approval." I generally count myself in the latter camp, unless a client overuses/abuses that latitude, or I am suspicious that she might.

• **What is the deadline?** Longer timelines don't necessarily mean a lower price, in light of what the workload is; however, tight deadlines warrant a premium.

Every one of these specifications depends on your particular client's needs. Don't assume anything. If you don't know an exact answer or basic range, ask. (If you haven't memorized a fixed set of qualifying questions, start compiling a list based on the one above.) If the client seems uncertain, aim high. In addition, the estimate you present should list or otherwise address each of those components, even if you don't assign a specific dollar amount. (See Appendix I for an example of an estimate.)

Keep in mind that calculating the hours on some of those tasks may be challenging early in your freelance career. But each job you do, and every estimate you formulate, will provide you with increased perspective, accuracy and assurance that you'll be compensated appropriately for the given project—and you'll therefore have a better idea of what to charge the next time a similar project comes around.

Category 2 (Art and Voodoo): The Fudge Factors

Now we come to the art and voodoo aspects of estimating. The more daunting aspect of coming up with a quote often is taking into account some of the highly individual items that can't be defined in hours or put into a spreadsheet but that will have an impact on how much you charge:

• **How busy are you right now and during the proposed project period?** If you are busy, add a bit of a premium and see what happens—you might surprise yourself.

• **What's the overall economy like, and how well is the client's industry doing?** This shouldn't affect how much you charge, but it will undoubtedly affect the likelihood of your estimate being accepted.

• **How big is the client's company?** In general, a larger corporation is more likely to accept a higher rate. In fact, if you don't charge enough, the company may be suspicious that you're not qualified.

• **Is this a one-off project, or is there potential for additional business immediately or down the road if things go well?** Don't, however, fall into the trap of lowering your price based on promises that "there's more where this came from"!

• **Is this an existing client with expectations based on prior project pricing?** You probably don't want to get too aggressive with a price increase—unless your previous estimates turned out to be too low.

• **Does this client seem responsive and easy to work with, or is he needier than average?** One of my colleagues applies what she calls "an irritant surcharge"—a phrase I love.

• **Am I working with a single point person, or am I answering to several?** In the case of the latter, a more complicated project means more time—and you should budget for it.

• **What could securing this client and project mean for me in terms of my portfolio?** It's always nice to have a big brand for name-dropping purposes, or an exceptionally cool project to show off your skills. It's also beneficial to diversify into new industries and media. And a well-connected, high-visibility client could represent an enormous amount of referral business.

• **What is the shelf life of the project?** Freelancers commonly overlook this aspect of estimating. Inherently, something like a tweet or Facebook post is going to have less perceived value than a website or book, even if it takes you almost the same amount of time to write or edit it. (Let's face it; most tweets don't last as long as a piece of chewing gum.) A corporate tagline might be used for years, even if it's something that comes to you the moment you sit down at the computer.

• **Will I need to subcontract any of the work?** Assuming you will have to manage the subcontractor at least a bit, you will want to mark up this person's costs.

Now that we've assessed the details you need to consider, let's discuss three basic calculation techniques you can use to come up with your basic estimated figure—along with a couple of examples to illustrate.

The Add-It-All-Up Method. Just as it sounds, this is an exercise in raw number crunching. Add up the hours from Category 1, multiply this number by your hourly rate, and then take into account the variables from Category 2 to adjust your figures.

» EXAMPLE 1

Pete is a relatively new freelancer who's bidding on a simple, five-page website. Based on the conversation with the client, he'll be able to work with existing brochure materials, augmented with an hour-long interview with the company president to help set the tone. The writing, interview and revision process should take about 15 hours, which at his $75 hourly rate would mean $1,125. The turnaround time, however, is tight, and he's going to need to work late and maybe over the weekend to get it done. Adding 10% to his customary rate and rounding to the nearest $50, he decides to bid at $1,250.

» EXAMPLE 2

Experienced writer Jenny secured a brochure project with a client she's done work for before—and who she knows is high-maintenance and will probably require several rounds of revisions in addition to two interviews and an onsite meeting. The writing will only take about 6 hours, but the interviews, meeting and revisions could easily double that. Her calculation is that $1,200 (12 hours at a $100 hourly rate) should cover even the worst-case scenario, such as the addition of another interview, a meeting, or six or seven revisions instead of one or two.

The Per-Word or Per-Page Method. Although you should always go into a project with an understanding of how long the tasks and process should take, many experienced freelancers are eventually able to formulate a system based on word or page count, using history to serve as a shortcut and tweaked to the parameters of the project.

» EXAMPLE 3

Sydney charges anywhere from $3 a page to $8 a page for book editing, depending on whether a client needs a light, medium or heavy edit. The deadline is a month away, so she'll be able to work on the book after she completes the project she's currently working on. After reading a three-page sample and talking with the author, she recommends a medium edit—at $5.25/page, she bids $1,050 for the 200-page book.

» EXAMPLE 4

Bill gets a referral to a *Fortune 500* client from one of his existing clients. It's a huge opportunity: writing a whitepaper that will be presented at a national conference. While his initial instinct is to bid low in order to secure the job, the totals from Category 1 indicate it's going to be a substantial amount of work—and the company is in a thriving area of the software industry. In addition, he learned from his contact that the company uses one of the city's most expensive ad agencies to do most of its marketing and ad work. Not wanting to leave any money on the table, he estimates the job at $2.50 a word—less than what the comparable ad agency charges, but a considerable amount over his customary rate of $1.75 per word for whitepaper work. He doesn't tell the prospect those numbers, of course, but he uses them to derive an overall bid range.

————

The Client-Supplied Method. In many cases, the client will have a set rate within which you'll be expected to perform. When that happens, you need to do the math in reverse to see if the project is worth your while.

» EXAMPLE 5

Kari is considering pitching a feature story to a national sports magazine but is disappointed to learn that the publication pays only $0.20 a word, which is half the lowest rate she'll usually accept. Several factors make this assignment attractive beyond the fee, however: 1) It won't be a difficult story to write, since it's in her area of expertise and she has lots of contacts. 2) It would be a high-visibility name to have in her portfolio and could lead to more work. 3) It will give her a tax write-off for some travel costs that she was going to incur anyway. 4) She can probably rewrite and/or resell the piece elsewhere. Since it's been a couple of slow months for her, she decides to go for it—even though she'll make only $300 for the piece itself.

» EXAMPLE 6

When Nick gets a call from a past client who's changed jobs, he's excited. But when he hears that the hourly rate is $60 for 15 hours a month of magazine editing, he is torn—since that is $10/hour below his customary rate, and he's been pretty busy for the past few months. When he pencils it out, though, it would be awfully nice to have a steady $900 retainer to depend on each month and to smooth out the dips. Plus, it's an easygoing client who's a known quantity and with whom he has a good relationship.

Of course, you could always pick a number within a range provided by one of the popular rate surveys; however, if you take that approach, are you truly confident that it reflects the relationship between your business and the proposed project? When asked by the client, can you justify the specifics of the quote?

Ultimately, the best deals are the ones that make you and the client feel as if you're getting value from them. In the next chapter, we'll discuss strategic ways to present the numbers you've crunched above.

★★★

Do I Tell Someone My Hourly Rate?

In the freelancing business, particularly when you're starting out, there is no question more agonizing than "What's your hourly rate?"

Now, in the previous chapter, we spent quite a bit of time calculating your hourly rate—but that doesn't mean it's a number you need to promote or even disclose very often. For psychological reasons, if you have a high hourly rate, that can sound worse than the equivalent project cost for a freelance job cited as a lump sum. Savvy businesspeople are wary of open-ended arrangements, and they can mentally deal more easily with definitive quotes or ranges. (This is particularly true if they've been burned by a less-than-professional or slow freelancer in the past.)

That being said, if a client wants a specific, hard hourly number, I will provide that to her. If a client wants me to do three hours' worth of work at Z rate, I will do that for him. Again, the first principle always needs to be determining what is most appealing and persuasive to the given client—and that's a matter of listening to subtle (and sometimes not-so-subtle) clues during your conversations.

If your client requires an hourly rate, you need to state the number with confidence and without hesitation or apology: "My current hourly rate for new writing clients is $125." Practice saying it in the mirror, or on the car ride over to the initial client meeting. You need to convince yourself before you'll be able to convince someone else.

Handling the Vague Prospect

Estimating is all about precision, both to maximize your profitability as well as to protect yourself from problems down the line. So, when a client asks for a bid on ridiculously vague terms—"How much do you charge to write a 10-page website?" or "What's the cost to proofread my autobiographical novel?"—you are doing yourself a disservice to give an answer based on that data alone. It's much more professional to respond, "The more information you give me, the more accurate I can be about my estimate; without much data, I am going to need to bid in a broad range that might not be as helpful."

If you can't get an answer, you can obviously generate a very high, conservative estimate—because the critical element is that you should never commit to projects for which the worst-case scenario would be unacceptable. I wouldn't want to guess at how many words a small business's 10 website pages are going to be, nor trust an author's word that his novel "just needs a light edit." In essence, I always prefer to encourage the client to provide me more information before I cite any monetary figure.

Alternatively, you could pitch the idea of starting at an hourly rate for an initial period and creating a formal bid once the scope becomes clearer. Failing that, I'd leave the project to someone else. A proper businessperson should always be willing to fully inform a contractor before requesting a bid, and it's a major red flag if someone won't.

The Unseen Aspects of Ghostwriting Fees

I often get asked about ghostwriting rates, and for starters, let's just say this: It's complicated, and arguably more about voodoo than either art or science. You'll find numbers cited on the internet from the low thousands into the six figures, a spread so broad as to be completely unhelpful. Ultimately, you'll need to charge whatever the market will bear, and recognize that an experienced ghost can command a much higher fee than a newbie. But as part of the calculation, you'll need to consider several concrete factors if you want to add ghostwriting into your toolbox:

• The length of the book, in terms of word count and page count.
• The deadline for the first draft and final, approved version.
• The amount of background research that needs to be done.
• If the content is already in some written form, or if the author will provide audio files that can be transcribed and edited, rather than starting from scratch.
• The amount of back-and-forth that can be expected in the editing process.

Many components of the calculation are unseen, however. Advances, royalties or credit will change the contract negotiation as well as the ghostwriting rates. In turn, those are affected by whether the book is going to be self-published or if the author has secured a name publisher. (In the latter case, royalties would likely have higher value—unless compared to a self-published author with a track record of success and an exceptional sales and marketing plan.) Quantifying the value of royalties and credit is well into voodoo territory, particularly if it's an author's first book and you don't know how well it will sell. Freelancers know all too well that fame doesn't pay the mortgage as well as fortune does.

Finally, both parties need to go into any ghostwriting arrangement with 100% transparency (pun intended) and understanding of the roles and goals. I have ghostwritten tons of articles, speeches and books, but I've also turned down more opportunities than I can remember. Skilled ghosting costs far more than most inexperienced authors realize. And because of the extraordinarily high investment in time and energy for such projects, I recommend having a lawyer review the contract before you sign anything.

✳ Quick Tip: Ghostwriting Organizations

If you're interested in learning more about the finer points of ghostwriting, check out these organizations:

• The International Association of Professional Ghost Writers: iapgw.org
• Association of Ghostwriters: AssociationOfGhostwriters.org

CHAPTER 4

A Strategic Approach to Presenting Persuasive Bids

If you've come from a corporate background, where someone else was doing the selling, the moment when you make the first move—presenting your offer—can come with more than a dollop of anxiety. Did you price correctly, or did you shoot too high or too low? Did you forget something that you'll regret? Have you interpreted the client's needs correctly? Will the customer accept your estimate on the first shot, or are you headed to Haggletown?

The good news, as with most aspects of freelancing, is that the proposal process gets more intuitive over time. You will figure out your sweet spot. This chapter addresses some of the primary methods of presenting a bid in a way that persuades a client to do business with you. (In Appendix I, you'll find a sample estimate based on an actual, successful project bid.)

First, though, let's discuss some of the basic principles you need to keep in mind, regardless of which route you choose:

• **The best clients buy on value, not price.** The priority of savvy clients is on what you can do for them; the price is important, but secondary. (This is also a great argument against pricing by the hour—unless you have a nosebleed hourly rate that conveys superstar status, and so clients believe they're getting a bargain on a flat fee.) The converse is true, too: The worst clients buy on price, not value.

• **An estimate is a piece of communication.** Your pitch should be clean, professional, distinctive and easy to understand—not just an email or Word doc with the project name and a dollar figure.

• **Granularity is essential.** By covering all the details in your formal proposal, you are not only protecting yourself, you are conveying to clients that you listened carefully and understand their specific needs and deadlines. That gives you psychological leverage (and therefore negotiating leverage).

• **Respond within 24-48 business hours.** First, you may be in competition. Second, think about how antsy you get when you bid out a home improvement project and don't hear back from the contractors in a timely fashion. Tell the client when you're going to respond, and then deliver accordingly (or even earlier than you promised!).

Eight Basic Ways to Present Your Offer

Sometimes clients will specify the type of estimate they'd like to receive; if they don't, it will make you sound businesslike if you ask what they prefer. There are, however, numerous ways to spin the same information—it's not just a matter of "I'll do this and you pay me that."

Regardless of which format you choose, there are two key aspects to formulating your bid:

- You need to ensure that you are calculating the estimate in a way that is profitable for you and that reflects the skill set and professionalism you'll bring to the project.
- You have to put yourself in your clients' shoes: What type of estimate will give them the confidence that you offer significant value for their money, will do the job well and will treat them fairly?

---

❶ Per Word/Page — This is by far the simplest method of conveying your price, and theoretically, you can use this way for just about any type of writing or editing project. (Of course, if you've been assigned a magazine article, the editor will dictate this to you, rather than the other way around.) *Note: For people who are outside the publishing or marketing/advertising world, it may appear we're talking in a foreign language here. If this applies to you, I suggest you convert the per word/page cost into one of the other strategies that offer an overall project price estimate.*

Persuasiveness factor: ★ out of five

ADVANTAGES
- This rate is easy to calculate.
- This rate is common and is listed in most pricing charts.
- If clients are setting the prices, you rarely need to negotiate.

DISADVANTAGES
- You will need to know the precise specs ahead of time.
- Your rate may sound high to inexperienced clients or to people outside of publishing/marketing/advertising.
- Page size or quality can vary dramatically.
- This kind of sales pitch is not persuasive.

BEST FOR
- Fast writers and editors.

---

❷ **Per Hour:** As with per word and per page rates, this is pricing at its simplest, and you can use this method with almost any project. *But be forewarned—only a small percentage of clients want to purchase this way, particularly for an initial project before you have developed a relationship. Again, seriously consider converting your total-hour calculation into one of the other strategies.*

Persuasiveness factor: ★ out of five

ADVANTAGES
- The price is easy to convey.
- This rate is common and is listed in most pricing charts.
- It is useful for open-ended/ongoing projects that won't allow a firm bid or estimated range.

DISADVANTAGES
- It's counterproductive if you're fast.
- Your price may sound high to inexperienced clients.
- You need to take into account the client's "maintenance level."
- You need to track your hours carefully.
- This is not a persuasive sales pitch, unless it's what the client is asking for.

BEST FOR
- Small jobs.
- Big jobs with a healthy budget and a trusting client.
- When the client specifically requests it.

❸ **The Car Sales Gambit:** When you walk onto an auto dealership lot, you're presented with low-, medium- and high-priced options. In many cases, a freelancer can apply the same principle—providing a variety of price structures and service levels for a given project. The mere fact that you've given clients choices (and the illusion of control) can be a motivator.

Persuasiveness factor: ★★★★ out of five

ADVANTAGES
• The lowest price becomes non-negotiable; hagglers need to go elsewhere.
• The medium option becomes more attractive in relation to the highest option, and you can price this option for profitability.
• You can price the highest level lucratively, since the client has self-identified as someone who wants all the bells and whistles.

DISADVANTAGES
• This pricing structure is somewhat more complicated to assemble and customize.
• This method can be confusing to the novice client who doesn't want choices.
• It is not suited for all projects.

BEST FOR
• Experimenting within your market.
• Transparently raising prices on your services.

❹ **The Pie in the Sky:** Behind closed doors, I call this the "frivolous bid," which I use when I get a request for something that I'm not terribly interested in or when I'm really busy but would be willing to do it at a way-above-market price. *Note: You should use this method sparingly and only with over-the-transom business—not existing clients who are familiar with your pricing structure and might be upset by a way-out-of-line bid.*

Persuasiveness factor: ★ out of five

ADVANTAGES
- This is ridiculously lucrative if the client accepts the offer.
- If clients like your work, it can lead to additional high-profit jobs with them or people they refer to you.

DISADVANTAGES
- If the offer isn't accepted, you've burned a bridge.
- Money doesn't change the fact that you're uninterested or overwhelmed.

BEST FOR
- When you're already maxed out.
- When you just don't care, but the money would be nice.

---

❺ **Retainer:** In some cases, generally after you've developed a solid relationship with a client, it makes sense to create a regular monthly payment rather than piecemeal invoices every week—it can make life easier for both parties. *Note: A retainer is usually not a good method for a first pitch unless the prospect specifically brings up the topic.*

Persuasiveness factor:
★ **out of five** for a new client; ★★★★ for a loyal client

ADVANTAGES
- This method offers steady, predictable income for you.
- It offers the client easy accounting and an exact budget impact.

DISADVANTAGES
- You need to track your time carefully to address months you're over or under.
- This can require renegotiation if your workload always exceeds or falls short of the agreed-upon figure.

BEST FOR
- Long-term clients.
- Clients whose needs are consistent.

---

❻ **Firm Bid:** This is likely the most common type of bid presentation. You give a number based on the project description, and then the client says yes or no. Easy-peasy, right? Well, the challenge is that you are pinned to a number, which can then become a negotiating target—with nowhere to go but down. It's also problematic with regard to scope creep—when a client adds new tasks that weren't addressed in the initial estimate.

Persuasiveness factor: ★★ out of five

ADVANTAGES:
• This cost is easy to convey.
• It falls within common practice.
• Clients know the exact budget impact.
• This can be lucrative if you aimed high.

DISADVANTAGES:
• Clients may reject the offer outright.
• Clients may try to negotiate the price down.
• You can fall prey to scope creep.

BEST FOR
• When clients request it.

---

❼ **Not-to-Exceed Estimate:** A slightly more advanced version of the firm bid, this method adds a bit of persuasive flexibility into the equation. The key here is that you're telling clients the most that a project could cost them, while teasing that it might come in lower. As a result, you can safely price this marginally higher than the firm bid, while psychologically making it much less likely to result in negotiation.

Persuasiveness factor: ★★★★ out of five

ADVANTAGES:
• This method makes clients feel comfortable/confident.
• It encourages clients to be efficient and easy to work with.
• It can be more profitable than the firm bid, even if you come in lower than the estimate.
• The client knows the upper limit of the budget impact.

DISADVANTAGES:
- You need to make sure the not-to-exceed price is high enough to cover all possibilities.
- You can run into scope creep.

BEST FOR
- Skittish or budget-focused clients.
- First-time users of freelance services.

AND THE MOST PERSUASIVE PRACTICE IS...

❽ Estimated Range: This is by far my preferred way to present a bid, and I learned this strategy from an experience with a contractor. My family had purchased an old ranch home with a disaster of a kitchen that was a notch beyond my DIY skill set. After receiving three bids to bring things up to code and into the 21st century, we chose the person who seemed most trustworthy. Bob the Builder wasn't the cheapest, but he was the only one to provide an estimated range along with a comprehensive assessment of what needed to be done. (The other two offered firm bids and far less detail.) The final cost would depend on how difficult the job was once they started tearing things apart. Were asbestos-filled pipes lurking in the soffits? Did the wiring need to be replaced? Would the 1950s vintage plumbing disintegrate on contact? Six weeks and a cloud of gypsum dust later, we had a new kitchen. And, amazingly enough, the final bill came in several thousand dollars under the high end of the range. We were elated!

How does that apply to the freelancer who's bidding a job? Just like Bob, you're not always sure what you're getting into, and you're trying to make clients happy with the value they receive. Example: Instead of simply quoting a flat fee of $2,000, provide an estimated range of, say, $1,750 to a not-to-exceed $2,250—then, when the final total comes in at $2,100, you've made $100 more than you would have otherwise. Meanwhile, the client's perception is that you've come in $150 under her budget.

Persuasiveness factor: ★★★★★ out of five

ADVANTAGES:
- You're providing clients the comfort in knowing what the top, not-to-exceed cost will be.
- You're giving customers an incentive to be easy to work with (i.e., not going crazy with revisions or meetings).
- You're setting yourself up with a stronger negotiating position than a take-it-or-leave-it firm bid, because you're giving clients lots of detail and an option to remove certain elements if customers are price sensitive.
- You can nearly always rig it so that you come in less than the upper limit—so you can tout to clients that you were able to save some costs.
- Clients know the upper limit of the budget impact.

DISADVANTAGES:
- You need to make sure the upper end of the range is high enough to cover all possibilities.
- You may feel obligated to come in below the top fee.

BEST FOR
- Whenever you can use it.

Each of these eight options requires measures of art, science and voodoo. The dollar figure at the bottom of your estimate is important, but the way you communicate the numbers is where your creativity becomes most influential. In the scientific tradition, it's imperative that you experiment with different methods to see which one drives the best results for different types of projects and clients.

Why You Should NEVER Give an Off-the-Cuff Bid— With One Important Exception

You don't have to be in business very long before you'll have a conversation like this with an unknown, non-referred client who finds you from a random search on the internet:

Prospective client: "What do you charge for X?"

You: "Honestly, it depends on how many pages X is."

Prospective client: "Well, we're not really sure yet. Can you just give me a ballpark number on what you usually charge for X?"

You: "I'd be able to give you a much more accurate estimate with additional information. Do you have time to answer a couple of questions?"

Prospective client: "Well, we're still really early in the process and trying to figure out our budget. If you can provide me a basic number, I can take that back to the team."

This tire-kicker conversation can go on longer than a "Saturday Night Live" skit if you're not careful, but unfortunately, it's never funny. At the risk of seeming evasive, you really should never answer this question over the phone. If you do, there are three primary negative outcomes and a ton of permutations:

- You tell prospects a number that's too low, and then they're shocked when they get the actual, much higher "real" estimate.
- You tell them a number that's too low—and they want you to stick to it, as if it were some sort of ironclad contractual agreement.
- You provide a number that would be too high for the actual project parameters, and you scare off prospects.

Yes, your voodoo extrasensory perceptions might be working that day. You might happen to guess a number that works for the client, gets you the job and results in a lucrative project. The odds are heavily against this, however, and it's not worth the risk. You have no written documentation, just a verbal offer—the weakest, least persuasive position to be in. An unknown client with fuzzy information can be hazardous to both your business and your sanity. And there's no way to price the latter.

What's the exception to the rule? If an existing client—one you have an excellent relationship with and have done multiple jobs for—asks you to give an over-the-phone quickie quote, there's no reason to be coy. This individual knows you are an honest businessperson, and he or she is just trying to get some information based on limited facts, not trying to trick you into saying something you'll regret later.

Even so, you'll still want to provide a conservative range and offer a disclaimer: "Gary, those types of projects generally run from $900 to $1,400, but as you know it's going to depend on how long the actual document is, how many interviews I need to do and other factors. Sounds like a great opportunity, so please let me know when you have the details and I'll turn around a more accurate bid the same day."

What about Barter?

It probably won't happen often, but you'll occasionally run into clients who would rather trade their services for yours, or give a discount, than cut you a check. Personally, I've happily bartered with a chiropractor for free adjustments, as well as a local golf league so I could hit the links without pulling out my wallet. I hate the expression win-win, but that's what each of those negotiations was.

There are a number of caveats, however, when it comes to doing trade-outs:

- You still need to cut a professional, specific deal that spells out everything.
- Make sure you are getting the full value for your services, not selling yourself short.
- Uncle Sam considers the value of the bartered service as income, so talk to your tax advisor with regard to your own circumstances.

CHAPTER 5

Getting to "Yes"

With any luck, you sized up your prospect correctly; formulated a professional, detailed estimate; and addressed the client's needs at a price that fit just right. You signed the contract, received the deposit and can now put your remaining brainpower to creative use.

Then, there are those other times...

Now, there's a reason no-haggle car dealerships are a popular concept: Most people don't like confrontation—and negotiation can often imply a contentious circumstance that can make one of the parties feel as if they got a raw deal, or both feel equally unhappy. In freelancing, the dynamic can be complicated by the fact that there's no equivalent of a Kelley Blue Book on the value of creative services. (Worse, a client might cherry-pick a low-ball value from a fee chart that isn't valid for the project type or your skill/experience level.) Occasionally, you get a "no" that's so emphatic that there's not even room for negotiation. That's OK. Smile, thank the prospect for his time, and move on, with the knowledge that this project would probably have made you profoundly unhappy.

But here's the key: A business negotiation shouldn't be confrontational. Indeed, both sides should believe they're getting a fair exchange.

While researching this book, I met with one of my longtime clients, a print-shop owner in Phoenix. She is one of the smartest, most successful businesspeople I know, and her take on negotiation is founded on the Principle of Least Interest: "The person who has the least interest has the most power," she said. "If you come into our office to get printing or graphic design done, I don't have to work with you. I don't say that to be arrogant—it's just the idea that if you sit down with someone and you are doubtful you can create value at the price they're looking for, you can always say, 'I appreciate the fact that value is important to you, but it may not work for you.' People walk out and realize that you probably have something that they want! Then, you have a more respectful relationship."

Exactly so. You have the most power. You have something the other party needs. Think back on the basic concept that people don't actually buy on price. Rather, they buy based on emotion and the perceived value of what a given product or service is going to do for them—it's all about the art and voodoo. By nature, many of us are eager to please; particularly in a poor economy, we may be too quick to get to "yes." Dropping your rates not only decreases your profitability, it sets a precedent with clients. Moreover, playing hard-to-get (or at least harder-to-get) can psychologically raise your value in the client's eyes.

Common Objections

First, let's address some of the most common objections to an estimate, and how to handle them:

"I'm not sure your skills are what we're looking for." First, ask yourself if this is true. If it is, then you honestly are better off seeking a different project—the worst thing would be to overpromise and under-deliver after convincing the client to use you. If, on the other hand, you believe you truly are the right person for the job, it may be appropriate to have the prospect review some additional portfolio samples and emphasize how you've helped clients in the same sector or industry achieve success.

"I know someone who can do it cheaper." This and its equally ugly cousin, "My past freelancers have charged less," are the hallmarks of someone who is going to grind you on price. The little devil on your shoulder will be saying, "Well, then have them do it!" More prudently, you can use this as an opportunity to reiterate your superior skill set or talent, and how you're worth every dime, again citing the specifics of similar past successes. Keep in mind, you've been given an early warning sign that money will probably be an ongoing issue with this particular client.

"This is more extensive than what we had planned on doing." There's nothing wrong with this objection since it's not necessarily anything to do with price or your capabilities; use it as an opportunity to open a more in-depth discussion on how the client would like to approach the project.

"We've decided to go with another freelancer." Depending on how this is communicated—a brush-off or a sincere appreciation for your bid—the client may be open to working with you in the future. Express your eagerness to do so, and mention that, if the other freelancer doesn't work out for some reason, you'd be happy to jump into the void. Feel free to ask directly what the other freelancer offered that you didn't, which can help you hone your approach next time. Put the client on your "future contact" list, and reach out in a few weeks for a temperature check.

Silence. The first time you get a non-response, it's awful. When you get the 10th or 20th, you realize it's just part of the game. During your initial conversation, it's always advisable to ask the client when you can expect a decision on your bid; assuming you have done so, the day after the deadline has passed, it's appropriate to contact the client with a pleasant note expressing that you're ready to get going as soon as you've got the green light. If you don't have a date, give it a week. Still no answer? A few days later, you can try following up by phone, and a week or so later, try an email and a phone call. Be patient and polite, because you don't yet know the reason for the non-answer—plus, you have absolutely no leverage. After a few tries, send a final email note letting them know it's your last attempt to contact them. You're giving up trying, but not giving up hope. I once had someone contact me 18 months after I provided a bid!

Tweaking Your Terms

Even if the prospect doesn't say so explicitly, many objections equate to "Can you lower your price?" If you cannot convince a client that you do, indeed, offer the appropriate value for the rate, the next step is to tweak your terms. This is not some sort of automatic discount, however; it is a strategic process to maintain pricing integrity in alignment with the services you render. Obviously, it makes sense to give more latitude to a loyal client whose work style is a known

✳ Quick Tip: One More Reason Not to Rely on Discounts Alone

Bestselling author and former GE CEO Jack Welch commands a very high fee for his public speeches and gets frequent requests to do them for far less. His philosophy? Every time he gives a discount, it's unfair to customers who paid full freight.

quantity than to a newbie who's asking you to cut him a break. You can do the following:

Negotiate a decrease in service with a lower price. While not ideal, this is the simplest option in most cases. If you've given sufficient detail in your estimate, have the client line-item veto the least important items, and rework the estimate.

Ask the prospect to give you an acceptable budget figure. With a new number in hand, now you can re-quote what you can do for that price, or at your hourly rate. Yes, you're making less overall, but you haven't compromised your rate structure.

Ask for a time extension. In this case, you're not negotiating the price down at all, just the deadline. This can be particularly effective with a time-sensitive client; this client may suddenly discover that it's worth paying the full rate. Or, if the client agrees to an extension, you've taken some of the pressure off yourself.

Offer the client the option to use some of the work for other purposes. Without getting too much into the weeds on copyright law, a basic agreement gives the client the rights to use content for a given purpose at a specified price. Generally, you would want to upcharge for expansion of those rights—letting the client use your web copy to create a brochure or an ad, for example. But, in some cases, you could offer a specific other purpose at the same price, assuming no further work is required on your part.

Walk away from the deal. After trying one of the above approaches, you're still getting nothing but "I can't pay you that much." You have a decision to make: Is it worth dropping your fee to get the job? If the answer isn't an emphatic "yes," you may be stepping into a project you'll regret. (For perspective, it may help to revisit some of the "fudge factors" listed in Chapter 3.)

Given the above, you can see why the estimated range is such a powerful tool when it comes to negotiating: You can say something to the effect of, "I've crunched the numbers on your project, and I am confident that they're in the right range. I'm also confident that I'm the right person for the job. But, knowing that price is an issue for you, I'll do everything I can to keep the final invoice in the lower end of the range." Thus, you've stuck to your price range but offered the client the comfort of knowing you're looking out for her bottom line.

At the risk of retreating into a sports metaphor, people in creative fields are analogous to baseball players—some are superstars while others barely make it to the big leagues, but the vast majority toil away in the minors for smaller bucks. And far more play ball just for fun with the company softball team. A marginally talented player who wants to make a million bucks a year ain't gonna get it. One who has scads of talent, but who is underpaid, can always do a better job of negotiating.

For a freelancer, that means sticking to your guns. You have put time and effort into developing your skill set and experience, and you've developed a logical, defensible pricing schedule that makes sense for your business model. Why would you allow someone else to dictate what those numbers are?

✶✶✶

When a Client Tries to Renegotiate after the Fact

One of the more challenging situations occurs when work has commenced, but the client comes back asking to decrease the price or increase the amount you'll do for the same price. Of course, it's extraordinarily unethical to pull such a stunt, but it shouldn't affect how you operate. Calmly and objectively restate the terms of the agreed-upon parameters, and let the client know you'll need to stick to them to continue on the project.

If the client persists in haggling, cease work immediately, deduct the appropriate amount from your deposit and return whatever is left. In a worst-case scenario—the client tries to get a lower price after the work is completed—politely but firmly let the client know that you need to be paid in full. Otherwise, all files should be returned without being used for any purpose whatsoever.

CHAPTER 6

Why I Love Emergency Clients

There are a couple of times a year when clients suddenly find their to-do lists all at the same time. I prepare myself mentally for it, of course, and have plenty of strong coffee at the ready. There's often a rush two months before the holidays, then again the first few weeks of the new year—it's a deluge of projects that need to be researched, interviewed, written and approved in a day or two. It's stressful, but I have to confess that I like the adrenaline rush.

More important, I love the by-product: earning client loyalty for life while earning a higher-than-normal fee.

It cultivates a unique client bond when you pull a rabbit out of the hat. For my best clients, I will say, "Yes" 99.99% of the time and will figure out how to get it done. But I follow two rules: I do this ONLY for clients with whom I have a strong relationship, because I can trust they're telling the truth, and I do it ONLY at a premium price, for obvious reasons.

Oh, and lest I forget, I do the projects ONLY if they're generally non-rush. I don't want to get too close to someone who's in a constant state of emergency, or to encourage that behavior. If you've ever taken a lifesaving course, one of the first rules you learn is that, if a drowning person starts to take you under, get the heck away from him or her.

So, there's an important distinction here when it comes to putting on your last-minute superhero costume:

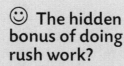

☺ **The hidden bonus of doing rush work?**
It's unlikely to require any revisions!

- I'm not talking about an over-the-transom prospect who found you on Google and who needs something done in a hurry. (As the old saying goes, "Poor planning on your part doesn't constitute an emergency on my part.") Handle such cases individually.

- I'm also not talking about "the client who cried wolf," for whom every single project is an emergency.
- I'm talking about a good client with whom you have a solid relationship and who happens to need a lifesaver.

That last bullet is key: These are clients who will brag about you without even being asked, in many cases leading to referrals. (Their referrals also tend to be high quality, too, because your best clients tend to network with equally solid businesspeople—and they'll rarely send you a dud.)

I remember well from my days as a managing editor when a freelancer would flake out, or when a story that was a complete piece of garbage came in, or when an ad salesperson would sell a last-minute ad that bumped up the magazine with an additional eight blank pages we had to fill. I knew specific writers who would come through in the clutch and who were regulars in my freelance stable.

As fellow freelance writer Stephanie Conner (TheActiveVoice.com) said to me, "Being an unflappable freelancer goes a long way." If you're willing to work that extra bit harder for clients or editors when they're in desperate straits, they're going to be eager to give you assignments and referrals long after the emergency has passed.

✳ Quick Tip: The Four Keys to Successful Emergency Projects

1. Make sure the scope and specifications are clearly defined. You cannot afford to have miscommunications.

2. Schedule or reschedule any other work to eliminate any impact to other clients. It would be shortsighted, not to mention poor business ethics, to sacrifice one relationship for another or to deliver less than your best possible effort.

3. Be realistic. You need to decline the project if it is truly impossible given the time allotted.

4. Fully inform clients in advance if there will be any rush charges. No one wants to be surprised with a whopping bill.

How Much Should I Charge for Rush Fees?

Ask 20 different freelancers, and you'll get 20 different answers to this question. Over the years, I've seen recommendations from 10% to a doubling or tripling of the regular price. There is no tried-and-true formula, because emergencies come in too many flavors: A next-day turnaround on a 300-word blog post isn't going to inflict the same pain as researching and writing a 2,000-word magazine story over a much-needed weekend.

Ultimately, the answer comes in the form of a sliding scale that you calculate on your own terms. Perhaps your minimum rush fee is 10% for a task that's not terribly taxing but that is needed faster than you'd usually perform the work, while something that requires putting other work on hold warrants an upcharge of 30%, 40% or more—as long as you can get the client to agree to it!

CHAPTER 7

Dealing with No-Pay and Slow-Pay Clients

A wise old man once told a younger me, when I was whining about something or other, "Son, 'fair' is something you enter your prize pig in."

No, it isn't fair when a client is slow to pay, or doesn't pay at all. But it is common, particularly in a down or sideways economy. I've never used a voodoo doll to get revenge; this is the one time where it's awfully tempting.

A recent *Wall Street Journal* article cited a stat from the Freelancers Union that 77% of their members have clients who didn't pay at least once. Frankly, that seems low, unless a lot of their members haven't been around very long.

The "Freelance Forecast" annual survey underscores how much of a problem no- and slow-paying clients are: It ranks #2, right behind "uncertainty" as the aspect of freelancing that freelancers dislike the most about the business. In addition, pay issues are the #1 reason that freelancers fire their clients.

So, how do you start that uncomfortable conversation with someone who's having trouble finding his wallet?

Here are some tips:

- Don't be afraid or embarrassed about asking for what you're owed.
- Try going straight to the accounting department if you're really getting the runaround.
- Let the client know, politely but firmly, that you're obligated to withhold future work till full payment is received.
- Offer alternative payment plans. Sometimes, offering the client the option of paying in two or three installments can help (and can engender goodwill), particularly if it's a small or startup company.

Here are a few other solutions, though they each come with potential pitfalls:

Assess late fees. With the right client, particularly one with deep pockets and a loose system, this can work. With others, assessing fees may get you labeled as high maintenance—and you may not realize it till it's too late. If you are going to charge fees for late invoices, this absolutely must be established and agreed upon at the outset, either in your estimate or contract, or both. And make sure you enforce the rules you put in place.

Offer incentives for quick payers. You can also try the opposite approach from late fees, which you can spin more positively: Offer a 3% discount for invoices paid within 10 days, for example. Just make sure you build the appropriate markup into your estimates.

Work with freelance job sites that handle the financial side for you. The benefit is that you're sure to get paid. The downsides are that you're letting someone else take a cut of your fee, they're setting what that fee is, and you're exposing yourself to a pool of additional competition.

Send a strongly worded letter with a cc: to your lawyer. Just seeing a legal firm being involved can often spur a laggard into action. You can up the ante by making it a certified letter with return receipt requested, enclosing all of the overdue invoices and a polite but firm letter. If it's a larger company, you may want to escalate to the CFO or even the CEO, if appropriate.

Send the invoices to collections. Recognize, of course, that you should use this tactic only after everything else has failed, and that you will need to give a cut of the action to the collections agency.

Sue the company in small claims court. This qualifies as a major escalation. I know some freelancers will fight to the death on even the smallest of invoices, but that isn't something I particularly want to get involved in. (Mercifully, I've never gotten skunked on a job large enough that would have made it worth the money and psychological capital to pursue.) Part of the problem is that the creative community is small, and you need to consider the ramifications as far as your reputation is concerned.

A Measured, Reasonable Approach

I've talked to enough freelancers over the years and experienced it myself: *The riskiest job is the first job you do with someone.* So, here are some overarching thoughts in addition to those above:

• **Be realistic.** If you're soliciting new business that isn't referral based, you need to accept that there will be slowpokes and scammers. You should be wary, too, when a so-so client refers business—because the prospect's expectations may be skewed. It's part of being in business for yourself. Don't spend the money before the check has cleared.

• **Request a deposit on new jobs and for existing clients who have had payment challenges in the past.** This serves three purposes: 1) It gets you some cash flow upfront. 2) It confirms that the client is serious. 3) It provides some negotiating leverage. If someone won't agree to pay a deposit, that is a major no-pay/slow-pay warning sign.

• **Be patient.** The best way to ensure you get paid on time is to work for people with whom you've developed a business relationship of trust. There are no shortcuts.

• **Don't get crazy.** I've seen a few people go to war on social media, in an attempt to smear a client who wasn't paying in proper fashion. While it may feel good at the time, keep in mind that other people—read, potential clients—are watching.

✶✶✶

Getting Skunked

A few years ago, I took on a referral for writing the content for a small website. The owner seemed nice enough, but her site was ghastly. I offered a modest bid, which she promptly accepted. I commenced on the website copy, and she seemed to be happy with the initial two pages. With the next few pages, however, warning bells started to ring. At this point, she wanted to know exactly how much her tally was and asked me to send an invoice.

Then I didn't hear from her. Then I sent a second notice, and a polite email asking when I could expect payment or if she'd like to break it up into two installments. No response.

Fast forward a few weeks. I called her, and again, as politely as possible, inquired about the status of the invoice. At which point she informed me that she had shown my invoice to another writer she knows, and this writer thought that it was too high, despite being what we'd agreed on.

After a bit of back-and-forth, I simply said, "You know what, Sandy, clearly we're not getting anywhere here. I think it's best if you just send me a check for what you believe you owe me. If that's $0, that's your prerogative, but as our contract dictates, you can't use the copy I've provided."

I'd already wasted my time; there was no sense in wasting further mental energy, and the piddling amount didn't make it worth pursuing legal action. But it was a stark reminder of why a deposit is an absolute must, even for the smallest of projects.

✳ Quick Tip: Warning Signs

You can't always know which clients are going to be challenging when the bill comes due, but these are a few indications:

- Extraordinarily tough negotiations about the price at the estimate stage
- Unwillingness to deliver a reasonable down payment before you commence work
- Trying to negotiate a lower rate after the agreement has been made or the job has started
- Hints or outright statements about being tight on budget or business being slow
- Inaccurate/unfounded complaints about the quality of your work
- Lack of responsiveness to emails/phone calls

When a Client Files Bankruptcy

Businesses fail, often without much notice—although chronic slow pay-ing can be an early indicator. If you find out a client has filed bankruptcy, your chances of being paid in full are, unfortunately, quite low. (This is yet another reason to always get a deposit before commencing work and to invoice promptly when you're done.)

The process for dealing with bankrupt businesses differs depending on the type of bankruptcy. USCourts.gov offers lots of information as well as the forms required, but the basics include the following:

- Cease all collection activity once you've been informed of the bankruptcy.
- File a proof-of-claim form with the court-appointed trustee.
- Get in line and sit tight.
- If and when you get paid, the money you earn is still income and you need to pay the taxes even if it's not the full amount due.

Recognize that bankruptcy can be a drawn-out process, and that you're just one of many people in the same situation. I once received a check nearly three years after the filing—I'd practically forgotten I'd even done the job!

CHAPTER 8

Low-Ballers and Nickel-and-Dimers

There are many reasons to reject low-paying freelance jobs, but first and foremost is this: You're devoting your valuable time on something when you could most surely spend your time better somewhere else. It's an opportunity cost.

Now, it's important to draw a distinction between low-ballers and nickel-and-dimers, though they're often related. First, let's deal with low-ballers, which I define as prospects who are bottom fishing or looking for a bargain. From a business perspective, it's a reasonable tactic; after all, most of us will shop around to find the best price on a TV, bed or airline ticket. Such prospects could be doing so because they legitimately don't have the budget to hire someone more expensive, or they could just be trying to spend as little as possible. A variation on the theme is the carrot-dangler: A prospect who promises a steady stream of work in the future if you'll just give a discount on the first project. (Don't be shocked when he turns out to be one-and-done instead.)

But it takes two to tango. A low-ball offer works only if someone on the other end will accept it. The only way to avoid getting low-balled is on the front end. You need to set your value properly—which goes back to the theories of proper pricing and estimating—and then you need to stick to that. Once a potential client makes a low offer, he or she isn't going back up, in the vast majority of cases. And the freelancer isn't the winner in a race to the bottom.

Furthermore, if every job you're pitching is accepted without a flinch or without an occasional "no," you may be getting low-balled without even knowing it.

Evolution into High-Maintenance Hell

Once acquired, a low-ball client will frequently evolve into a nickel-and-dime client—becoming high maintenance, always questioning whether something is necessary or whether it could be done more quickly or cheaper, or even requesting a decrease in price after the fact. A nickel-and-dimer is always asking for that little extra piece of your brain on the side, making it look innocuous enough that you won't notice.

Consider these five things about nickel-and-dime clients:

1. Are you getting your full hourly rate out of these brief interactions, even when you include the 5 minutes at either end to get into and out of a file, and the time that you spend communicating with such clients?

2. Do these tend to be emergency and/or last-minute projects, and if so, are you charging a premium?

3. Have you conveyed your frustration to the clients, and explained why piecemeal projects aren't in their best interest?

4. Could you find a polite/delicate way to ask clients to batch the multiple tweaky projects into a weekly single session or document?

5. Are you sending multiple invoices and getting a separate check for each, or are you sending a monthly or semi-monthly accounting of your time?

If you're honest about your answers, your next step is probably clear. Some freelancers set a minimum price for their work; that's one way to handle it. I tend not to draw such hard lines, because my experience has been that open communication and coaching can sell clients on the benefits of efficiency rather than piece-mealing everything. Quite often, they don't even realize they're doing anything wrong.

And as for those who don't care, release them back into the market with a clean conscience.

✶✶✶

A Word about Content Mills

You can't discuss low-ball rates without addressing content mills, but I don't view it as a moral issue. As much as I disdain the content mills out there, I don't believe they're doing anything but meeting a need for low-cost, low-quality content—filling space with words. Nobody is forced to work for them, so using the word "sweatshop" is a bit precious. These companies are purchasing the editorial equivalent of cheesy clipart, and successful freelancers aren't competing against that.

So, if you wish to look at content mills as a way to build your portfolio or to branch into topics that you'd like to exploit in the future, that is a business decision you have to make. But realize, as discussed above, that there's an opportunity cost to it. Hunting down a real, paying client might be more work but ultimately can generate more income, not to mention clips you'll be proud to have in your portfolio—as opposed to something that you have to explain or legitimize to the next prospect in your sales funnel.

CHAPTER 9

Working for Free

A few years ago, I had the good fortune to interview Chris Anderson, former editor-in-chief of *Wired* magazine and author of the bestseller *Free: The Future of a Radical Price*. But don't be fooled by the title—his point wasn't some hippy-dippy concept in which you give everything away and then you're magically able to feed your family with goodwill for breakfast and karma for dinner.

Indeed, in *Free*, Anderson makes an important distinction: "Abundant information wants to be free. Scarce information wants to be expensive." For example, his marketing plan included giving away several hundred thousand digital copies of his book in the early going—but if you wanted to hire him to speak to your company about strategic ways to incorporate his ideas, he charged a hefty fee.

How does this apply to creative freelancers? By and large, what you're producing for a client would be considered "scarce" information in Anderson's parlance: You are creating something unique and highly tailored for a specific purpose. In contrast, something you are creating for yourself—a blog, an ebook, tweets, etc.—might be considered an investment in marketing and promoting your business. You are giving away content to drive prospects to your premium, custom service.

Each of us will draw the line in a different place, depending on our business models and the opportunities presented to us. I know people who won't write a blog post for less than $100 and others who happily dispense words by the barrel in exchange for links. There is no right answer—just whatever makes your enterprise work.

That said, let's walk through a few of the most common create-for-free scenarios that freelancers encounter, and the strategic considerations involved in each:

Working on spec. Try to name another profession in which you can perform work without an official agreement or contract but simply in anticipation of getting paid. (Contests fall into the same category.) Yet, many freelancers risk being taken advantage of, doing significant upfront work, in the hope of scoring a check for a project or article. The vast majority of experienced freelancers won't go anywhere near spec work, with the following exceptions:

- If you have personally communicated with an editor and believe it's a pretty sure thing.
- If it's a market or publication you're trying to break into and are willing to take a risk.
- If the content is sellable somewhere else.

Blogging/guest blogging. We're all hoping to get discovered, right? But realistically, that magical moment when a post catapults you onto the national scene just doesn't happen that often. (Think about all the disgruntled Huffington Post bloggers who got nothing when the site got sold to AOL for $315 million.) Do it for love, do it to impress your clients with your brilliance, do it for links, do it for whatever reasons that seem valid to you—but be objective in assessing the business purpose and direct or indirect benefits that result.

For the exposure. This and its ugly cousin, "I'll give you bigger/more/ paying jobs in the future," are serious danger zones. In most cases, you should scorn companies or people who want to negotiate within this category of free. Sometimes, particularly for writers who are just starting out, having something published or printed can have implied value within your portfolio; but the last time I checked, my local grocery store doesn't take payments in "exposure." You absolutely must consider the opportunity costs when doing your analysis.

Test assignments. These are often a necessary evil—it's challenging to assess certain skills, such as copyediting or proofreading, from a past portfolio or even a before-and-after sample. Ideally, your professional portfolio and testimonials from past clients should be the main thrust of your sales pitch. If you are a new writer without any work in the prospect's industry, however, the prospect may want to get a bead on whether you're the correct person for the job. But if a test is part of the deal, you need to make sure of the following:

- It's a small sample of your work—just enough to make a decision.
- Contractually, the sample will not be used in any way, shape or form by the client unless you get the gig.

Charitable organizations. Volunteer work is a fine way to build your portfolio while giving back to the community. Really, there's no downside to doing this type of work for free, as long as you have set appropriate boundaries on your time and availability. Note that the IRS allows you to deduct unreimbursed, out-of-pocket volunteer expenses, but not the value of your time.

Friends and family. As a general rule, I don't do paid work for friends and family. My experience is that they expect too much for too little, and emotions play too much of a role—i.e., they're generally lousy clients. I will, however, do small projects as a favor and if I am not jeopardizing any paying work in the process. (If you are going to try to do work-for-pay in this category, you need to treat it in as businesslike a fashion as possible: contract, deposit, etc.)

Giving away content or services may have a place in your marketing plans, and the goodwill you foster may even help generate referrals. But I'm guessing you are reading this book because you want to improve your business: You need to start from the premise that you generally deserve to be paid for what your brain produces.

By agreeing to write or edit for free, you are making a statement about the value of what you've done, and you also are quite possibly forgoing an opportunity elsewhere. Don't let the voodoo outweigh the science. What if you spent those two hours making cold calls, sending emails or revamping your website? If there is little or no expectation of a measurable benefit, you need to be willing to stand up for yourself, and take your skills to a different market.

"The problem is there's so goddamn many writers who have no idea that they're supposed to be paid every time they do something."

—LEGENDARY SCIENCE-FICTION WRITER HARLAN ELLISON

CHAPTER 10

Give Yourself a Raise—With a Purpose

"You need to raise your rates!" is a common rallying cry in the freelance-o-sphere, and I believe it's often a reaction (or an overreaction) to all of the low-ball clients and content mills out there. So, your first step to giving yourself a raise is staying the heck away from cat-food-wage work and instead committing to finding projects commensurate with your current level or aspirations.

As you gain experience and expertise, your brain is worth more, though it requires a bit of science, art and voodoo to ferret out exactly how much. You'll occasionally hear someone extol the virtues of raising your prices 5-10% every year just for the sake of raising them, or creating a "minimum" price for a given type of project: "I won't write a blog post for less than $100." That seems to me to be a shotgun approach to business strategy rather than a scientific one. On the other hand, if you suspect you started out too low in your fee structure, a 25% one-time raise might make economic sense—and your best prospects, who expect to pay honest rates for excellent work, won't even flinch.

A lot of freelancers get awfully strident about absolutes in pricing; I'll admit that it took me a few years to find my sweet spot, but even when I started out, I wasn't cheap. (I couldn't afford to be, as I was the sole wage earner with a wife, two toddlers and a mortgage.) I've raised my rates numerous times simply based on increased demand, and because I've gained broad and specific knowledge about more industries. You can raise your rates, too!

Eight Reasons You Should Increase Your Prices

1. You're ridiculously busy, so busy, in fact, that you're spending all your time on projects and can't remember the last time you had to market yourself.
2. You rarely or never get turned down for a project based on price.

3. You hear or read about other freelancers who have comparable skills/ talent and who are successfully charging more for similar projects for similar clients.

4. You're aiming at a higher-end clientele or an industry that warrants higher prices.

5. You're cultivating business in a major metro area or internationally.

6. Your personal circumstances and budget have changed.

7. You've been in business for a few years and have thereby developed the skills and portfolio of someone who should be paid more.

8. You just want to experiment and see if it clicks.

Four Simple Ways to Raise Your Rates without Client Pushback

As far as how to increase your profitability through higher fees, here are four artful, strategic approaches to consider implementing when you want to give yourself a raise:

1. **The Grandfather Clause.** Existing clients get to stay at their current rate, but you quote new clients at a 10-20% higher fee, which avoids the client exodus that you'd be concerned about if you did an across-the-board raise. If you're in the business long-term, you'll eventually need to make the business case for raising prices for loyal clients, too. A strong relationship and good past results will make that conversation easier when the time comes.

2. **The Stealth Raise.** Think about it this way: If you're not a public utility, why would you ever announce a price increase or make a big deal about it? Obviously, this one is easiest to implement if you're calculating estimates rather than working on an hourly or per-word basis—just build in another 10% (or whatever) for yourself in every new quote. As long as it's a modest increase, you're the only one who will ever know.

3. **The Circumstantial Increase.** You don't have to permanently restructure your pricing, of course. Instead, put a hefty premium on jobs during busy times or during the holidays. Consider it to be like giving yourself overtime or like a perk of doing business when you'd rather play with your new toys.

4. The Rate Sheet Swap. Personally, I don't provide a price sheet on any of my websites, but some freelancers swear by them. So, this would mean simply uploading a new price structure for people to see. You'd want to have a conversation with existing clients so your new prices don't come as an unpleasant surprise; you also should consider grandfathering them for a defined period so they can plan their budgets.

Although I'd love to think we should all be earning $300 an hour, reality dictates that you need to recognize the relationship between your talents, the demand for those talents and the market rates people are willing to pay for a given project. Raising your rates successfully is about understanding those factors from a business perspective.

★★★

The Prospect Who Expects a Deal

Sometimes, potential clients may have a preconceived notion of your fees because existing clients who are in the lower end of your price structure have referred you. ("Oh, sure, Jenny McWriter did my brochure for $500!") My feeling on that is you can't worry about it. If prospects are salivating at bargain-basement prices and suffer sticker shock, that's their issue, not yours. You must always price yourself objectively based on the project at hand.

If a prospect tries to say, "You did it for my friend for $500 and you're telling me $1,200?" you need to be ready for an answer that explains how:

- You can solve his problem.
- You'll make his project great.
- You're worth every penny.
- This is a different project, perhaps more challenging/time consuming, and not directly comparable.

If someone wants to challenge you on price, that will probably be an ongoing issue. A little negotiation is fine, but you always need to heed the voice in the back of your head if you get the feeling that a prospect will be difficult.

✶✶✶

Applying the Freelancer's "P/H Ratio"

I recently participated in a Twitter chat hosted by the Editorial Freelancers Association, and the topic turned to raising rates: "What if you have tons of work but aren't making much money? What should you do if you're charging too little for your time?"

Perhaps a bit flippantly, someone tweeted, "Charge more!"; I rejoined with "STAT!"

But upon further reflection, as much reflection as a fast-moving Twitter chat allows, I added, "Dump your worst client on an annual basis." To which the moderator responded, "How do you choose your worst client?"

Ah, now we're on to something. How do you identify your worst client? My gut reaction was that it's your lowest-paying one, but that's not true. Your worst client is—drum roll, please—the one with the *least favorable pay-to-hassle (P/H) ratio.*

For example, your lowest-paying client might offer interesting projects or pieces that look great in your portfolio, or the client might offer a wellspring of referrals that make it a more lucrative relationship than what shows up in QuickBooks. So, my equation includes the following factors:

- **Pay.** Does the client pay well? Does she pay promptly, or are you always chasing her?

- **Project quality.** Is it work you enjoy? Is it creative work that you're proud to have in your portfolio to attract new clients, or is it something you'd never admit to having done?

- **Maintenance level.** Is the client pleasant to work with or does he require lots of handholding/revisions/weekends?

- **Ancillary benefits.** Do you get referrals from her? Does she provide testimonials or share your social media postings? Does she offer discounts on her company's products and services?

- **Self-education.** Is the client teaching you something that you couldn't learn elsewhere and that will be financially beneficial to you in the future?

No two clients are the same, and some of the items above may be more important to you than to others when it comes to calculating a

P/H. (Personally, pay rate weighs pretty heavily.) And while you may not necessarily want to dump your worst client, it's worth having perspective in order to take corrective action: You can effectively raise your rates by eliminating clients whose maintenance levels outweigh the checks they scratch out with your name on them.

CHAPTER 11

Check, Please!

During my childhood, my dad was a traveling salesman, so I grew up thinking a paycheck wasn't a normal thing—in fact, a check was cause for celebration, usually accompanied with a cheap bottle of André Cold Duck. (I can still taste the awful stuff in my mind. Ugh!)

I didn't fully comprehend the full impact of an uncertain income, though, until I ventured out on my own after a decade in corporate life. I vividly remember the anxiety it caused when former coworkers would ask me, "What are you going to do without a paycheck?" The truth is, at first, I didn't really know the answer, but I knew I would figure it out. Not long thereafter, it became very clear: One of the sweetest moments in a freelancing career is the day you walk down the driveway and your mailbox contains not just one check, but two or three!

Don't Overlook Perception

So, you've completed the projects and articles, and you want the checks to start rolling in. Some companies will have you submit an invoice form that they've created, which is fine, but it's far more likely that you'll have to create one on your own. In my view, an invoice is one of the most important pieces of communication in your arsenal—a perfect opportunity to under-score your professionalism with a blend of science, art and voodoo.

How can you use invoices to improve a client's perception of your business? Well, several oft-debated topics enter into the mix:

Accounting program vs. Word/Excel. Sure, you can squeak by with something from the Microsoft Office Suite, but as a former editor, I can tell you that screams "amateur" within many corporate circles. (Not that you'd get paid any slower or less, but still...) In contrast, programs such as QuickBooks or FreshBooks give you a more customized look—includ-ing your logo, font and a clean format and design in a .pdf—and they offer other tools to help manage your freelance finances. Honestly, it is a worthwhile investment in your marketing image.

Employer Identification Number (EIN) vs. Social Security Number (SSN). There's no empirical proof that an EIN will get you paid more quickly, but it's indisputable that it establishes you in clients' (and, equally important, in their accounting departments') minds as a business vendor. Moreover, it keeps your SSN from inadvertently getting into the wrong hands, and gives you peace of mind. The EIN application takes just a few minutes to complete and can be found online at irs.gov.

Business name vs. your own name. Again, this puts you in the business category when a check needs to be written out to "Acme Content Services" rather than just "Pat Doakes." How to choose between a DBA, LLC, S Corp or other formation is beyond the scope of this book, but a search on your home state's government website will get you started on the necessary forms, fees and processes. Although it will depend on your state, it's often a DIY situation, no lawyer required.

Business bank account vs. personal account. With a formally established business and an EIN, you can march down to your local bank or credit union, start up a business account and get a set of business checks and deposit slips. Not only does this make it easy to separate your business and personal finances when it comes time to file your Schedule C with our friends at the Internal Revenue Service, you will find it drives a certain measure of psychological pride: Yes, you're a real business!

What if you're freelancing only part time? Is it really necessary to deal with the time, cost and bureaucracy to accomplish these steps? Certainly you can make a valid argument either way, and some successful full-time freelancers use their own names, SSNs, Word invoices and

✳ Quick Tip: Keeping It Legal

Federal and state tax authorities are cracking down on companies that evade taxes by hiring freelancers while treating them like employees. Having a business name, bank account and EIN underscores that you're an independent contractor.

regular bank accounts. Unless writing and editing is more of a hobby than a business for you, however, I recommend taking a more formal approach and capitalizing on the numerous advantages.

Invoice Essentials

As with your estimate and proposal, your invoice should include sufficient detail about the project and the services you performed, as well as the specific dates during which you performed them. Particularly if your contact isn't the person processing the invoice—instead, it's some nameless accounting drone in the bowels of the building—the invoice will convey that this was an important piece of official business that demands attention. A few of the other details that warrant discussion include the following:

Invoice number. Even if a client doesn't ask for or require a numbering system, start one and use it. (Accounting programs will do this for you, and this is another mark in the plus column for automation.) It's essential for tracking what's been paid—and particularly handy for sorting out multiple check stubs from the same entity with the same dollar figure.

Payment terms. It's common to think of default terms such as "payable on receipt" or "net 30" as good enough. But an interesting survey by FreshBooks (FreshBooks.com) indicated that "days" is a more effective word than "net," and that invoices due within 21 days got paid sooner than those with longer or shorter deadlines. Curiously enough, the ol' standby "Payable on receipt" was among the worst choices, perhaps communicating an air of "whenever you feel like it" if you don't specify a due date.

Deposit credit. Assuming you asked for and received a deposit before commencing work, don't forget to credit accordingly when sending out the final invoice.

Additional costs. The invoice stage is a disastrous time for surprises. If your contract included rush fees and the client agreed to them, fine. If the client changed scope and was informed of the financial implications of the extra work, that's fine, too. But don't expect to load up on unexpected fees and not get an angry phone call. Put yourself in the client's shoes, and you can understand why.

Statement about late fees or credits for fast payments. Again, this should be only as previously defined and agreed to.

Polite closer. The FreshBooks survey also found that including a phrase such as "Thank you for your business" or "Please pay within 21 days" increased the percentage of invoices paid by more than 5%. Talk about positive voodoo!

When Should You Invoice?

The short answer is "as promptly as possible after the client approves the project or article." Your more diligent clients will even prompt you to send an invoice, which is always a relief. Realistically, however, jobs may straggle on with minor edits or additional tasks after you have completed 95% of your work, or sometimes the project is waiting on processing by a third-party graphic or web designer before you can invoice. If you're unsure, the best route is to contact the client with a friendly phone call or email, asking if it's OK to send a full or partial invoice now that things are pretty much wrapped up.

When Should You Follow Up?

If you've gone the full number of business days cited in the payment terms plus a couple of days for mail to make the trip to your mailbox, a polite follow-up is appropriate. Nonetheless, patience is a virtue: In my experience, some of my highest-paying clients will take 30 or 60 days, regardless of my terms, and I've eventually learned their rhythm after I've done multiple projects for them—so I don't panic or feel a need to escalate. (For further strategies to handle more serious lateness issues, please review Chapter 7, "Dealing with No-Pay and Slow-Pay Clients.") Note: If you've written an article for which the terms stipulated "payment on publication" rather than "payment on approval," remember you're at the whim of the publication's schedule, and a follow-up plan should reflect that.

Ultimately, the best things you can do to ensure getting paid promptly are to do your due diligence on the front end when vetting clients, to execute projects with the utmost professionalism and to invoice in a timely fashion. And don't forget to crack open a bottle of your favorite adult beverage the next time you get two checks in one day—shoot me an email, and I'll join you in a virtual toast.

★★★

Creating a For-Your-Eyes-Only Rate Sheet

Immediately after invoicing is also the perfect time for a quick self-assessment:

- How close was your estimate to the actual workload the project entailed?
- Did the client require more or less handholding than you anticipated?
- Were there problems with scope creep, additional rounds of revisions or hard-to-reach resources?
- Next time, what questions could you ask to help you formulate a more accurate estimate?

But the most important question you need to ask is this: **Would I do this project for this client at this price again?** If you find yourself answering, "No," it's either because your estimate was faulty (good client/ bad price), or it's a client you don't care to work with in the future (bad client at any price).

In the latter case, your solution is simple: Cut 'em loose—politely, professionally and after the check has cleared. There's no need to pre-emptively tell the client you're severing the relationship, but do so the next time that client contacts you.

In the good client/bad price scenario, re-do the math: What *should* you have charged? It's the same principle as an architect uses in construction; after a project is complete, the architect draws an "as-built," creating an accurate record of the existing conditions. In addition, you need to consider whether you would have charged this particular client more (e.g., I need to use my hourly rate plus 10% in the future), or whether you would always charge more for this type of project (e.g., my ghost-writing rate needs to be higher).

Earlier, I discussed the pros and cons of posting your rates publicly. Even if you don't plan to include dollar figures on your website, you will save yourself a lot of time and rework by compiling an internal, for-your-eyes-only rate sheet. As Mark Twain said, "History does not repeat itself, but it does rhyme."

It's as simple as creating a spreadsheet or Word doc table that includes these elements:

- Project type (writing, editing, ghostwriting, proofing, design, etc.)
- Price range per word/page
- Price range hourly
- Price range project (high/low)
- Questions to ask/other factors to consider
  - New client vs. existing client
  - Deadline
  - Quantity of research, interviews, revisions, meetings, etc.
  - How to charge this specific client in the future

Voilà: The next time a project that's similar to something you've done before comes in, you've got a head start on the questions you need answered, the time it will take to do a given task and the approximate amount you should charge. If it's a long time between projects for a given client, this cheat sheet can jog your memory about the items you needed to adjust. And each time you do a new project of a given type, and as your rates rise, adjust your figures to reflect reality.

What about Direct Deposit?

If this option is available, take it. There's no downside, you'll get paid faster, and you'll save on trips to the bank and on stamps and envelopes.

✳ Quick Tip: Two Steps After You've Been Paid

I mentioned the importance of a thank-you closer in your invoice, but the smart freelancer has two more essential touch points after the check is received: The first is a handwritten thank-you note to the person who hired you. Whether it was a small job or a major one, and even if it wasn't all smooth sailing, take a few minutes to write a note on your logoed business stationery to acknowledge that you've been paid. Thank him or her for the opportunity to work on the project—and express your interest in collaborating again in the future. It's a personal touch that will put you above the crowd.

The second step, most appropriately taken a week or two after the thank-you note and assuming the job went well, is to politely request referrals and a testimonial. Successful freelancers will tell you that referrals are by far the best way to get new business: As mentioned earlier, great clients tend to network together, plus you get the benefits of a warm call when you make your pitch. And a testimonial from a satisfied customer posted on LinkedIn and your website offers social proof to prospects that you will deliver for them, too.

CHAPTER 12

Protecting Yourself

We've all heard the refrain that you need to treat your freelancing like a business. That's not to say that you shouldn't be massively creative or just plain goofy much of the time, but rather that sometimes you can't act that way. Part of that is being responsible for yourself—and protecting the income that you've worked so hard to earn—when things don't go according to Hoyle. Yeah, I'm talking about insurance.

Health insurance. The rising cost of health insurance is a major sticking point for us solo practitioners. It's worth the time to investigate your options and even to revisit the details of your current plan regularly. Back when I first went freelance, for example, I discovered personally that COBRA was far more expensive than what I could get on my own for the coverage I wanted. With all of the changes taking place in healthcare laws—i.e., getting more complicated and expensive—freelancers need to be vigilant.

Disability income insurance. Today's cheery thought: You're much more likely to have a period of disability than you are to die. (Yet many of us have insurance to protect against the latter but not the former.) According to the Life and Health Insurance Foundation for Education (LifeHappens.org), "Nearly one in three women can expect to suffer a disability that keeps them out of work for 90 days or longer at some point during their working years. For men, the odds are about one in four. And one worker in seven can expect to be disabled for five or more years before retirement." The good news for freelancers is that we're in a low-risk field and premiums are relatively cheap. I've owned a policy for several years and, while I hope never to use it, it helps me sleep at night.

Errors and omissions insurance. You may have to show proof of this—also known as professional liability or publishers/media liability— if you do contract work for a larger company; you might also be able to get a waiver from the legal department since your contract is the final "sign off" on the content of any given project. If it turns out you need a policy, your best bet is to turn to a trusted insurance advisor who specializes in the field, such as Granite Insurance Brokers (Publiability.com), or to organizations such as the Freelancers Union (FreelancersUnion.org) and National Writers Union (nwu.org), which offer members insurance to protect against common legal threats.

Disclaimer: I'm not an insurance professional, I don't play one on TV, and the range of options that might apply to your business is highly individual. I'm providing the above opinions to get you thinking about and researching the topic as it applies to your business, not because I want to make specific recommendations. What you want, need and can afford must ultimately strike a balance with your risk tolerance and life circumstances.

But I will say this: When you consider that these are the types of insurance that an employer would purchase on your behalf if you were a full-time employee, isn't it in your best interest to take a serious look at how well you're protecting yourself?

CHAPTER 13

Your Go-to-Hell Fund

Personal finance gurus will tell you that building up an emergency fund of three to six months' worth of income should be a priority, and I agree. You never know what's going to happen to you, and you need to be able to pay the bills.

Running your own business has its advantages, but assuming you want to retire or at least dial back at some point, you also want to make sure you're setting aside your monetized brainpower in a retirement vehicle, whether it's a Roth IRA, SEP IRA, Solo 401(k) or other plan.

A go-to-hell fund, however, addresses financial security from a different perspective: It's about improving your personal voodoo, having control and taking daily action.

When I started my first job, my dad advised me to have enough money stashed away to escape a bad, negative or unproductive situation. Which is precisely what I did, quitting an aggravating job in order to ride my bike across the country. (I didn't make it, alas. I got run over by a guy who fell asleep at the wheel of a pickup truck in Montana.)

At the time my dad said it, I understood the concept purely in terms of being an employee and being able to tell a boss, "I'm out."

What I've found is that, for freelancers, his advice is even more important. The key is this: Your go-to-hell fund not only allows you to manage and/or extricate yourself from bad clients and situations, it enables you to avoid them in the first place. It's not something to be used on a whim; it's a business tool with strategic purpose:

- You can say "no" to freelance work without worrying about paying the bills.

- You don't need to take jobs out of desperation and therefore can negotiate from a position of strength. (That's also a morale boost.)

- You can dump bad clients without hesitation, which frees you up to attract more of your favorite freelance projects and to work harder for your good clients.

- You can set better boundaries with your good clients when they're starting to become too large a percentage of your business and limiting your diversity.

  It's a tough economy out there for a lot of freelancers, and saving money on top of everything else can seem like a tall order. But it comes down to choices: Either you build wealth to control your own destiny, or other people and projects will control it for you.

✳ Quick Tip: Three Ways to Start Your Go-to-Hell Fund Painlessly

- Commit 10% of each check, without fail, to a dedicated savings or brokerage account.
- Commit one big project a year that's purely for your go-to-hell fund—this works even better psychologically if it's a job you don't really like!
- Commit one four-figures-annually client to be your designated go-to-hell "sugar daddy."

CHAPTER 14

Final Thoughts

As I wrote at the outset, pricing your skills correctly is essential to having your clients and prospects value them properly. I sincerely hope the strategies in this book will help you to strike the appropriate balance in the day-to-day business of freelancing and to monetize your brain in the way you imagined you could but couldn't quite formulate.

I'll leave you with four final big-picture thoughts that are keys to my own freelance success:

Live below your means. I've been discussing the ways to make more money and to increase your profitability, but "living below your means" is an important corollary to that. A freelancer who is living check to check simply isn't positioned to make sound decisions. One who has money saved—and, yes, a healthy go-to-hell fund—has all the self-confidence needed to make the right decisions. In the words of legendary banker J.P. Morgan, "Take waste out of your spending; you'll drive the haste out of your life."

Heed the 80/20 rule. If you take an objective look at the Pareto principle (i.e., 80% of the effects come from 20% of the causes) you'll likely find that it applies to your freelancing business. About 80% of your income will likely come from 20% of your clients, and about 20% of your income will come from 80% of your clients. But this isn't just a math problem: The keys are to identify those top clients—the ones who assign you work regularly and pay you well and on time—and to cultivate more of them through marketing and referrals. They're the ones who already understand and believe in your value, no further convincing required.

Diversify, diversify, diversify. In a similar vein, you are exposing yourself to significant risk when you rely on one or two clients to provide you with a majority of your income. What would happen if they went out of business, hired full-time staff members to replace you or simply stopped calling? Even if you are focused within a niche, branching out is a prudent business move to insure against a downturn within specific client companies and their industries as a whole.

Don't judge yourself solely by financial results. I've written more than 20,000 words here about the merits of calculating and getting paid an honest wage for your labors. Your overall freelance enterprise, however, is vastly more than that: You are pursuing your creative aspirations while helping other individuals, companies and organizations achieve their own goals. As William Rosenberg, founder of Dunkin' Donuts, put it, "My father taught me that reputation, not money, was the most important thing in the world." Reputation, in turn, drives the referrals that can make your life a whole lot more pleasant—and profitable.

There is no one-size-fits-all way to price and estimate your fees, nor to negotiate and collect them—which is why I've offered such a wide variety of options and ideas for your consideration. The science of the process is about running the numbers and testing hypotheses. The art is about using your creativity to paint a picture in your clients' minds about how talented and pleasant to work with you are, and the value you deliver. On the other hand, the voodoo is really about understanding the unseen elements that exist in the gap between the two. With time, experience and persistence, you can be confident you'll develop the strategies that work best for you and your clients.

✷✷✷

Your Success Stories Wanted!

Have you used one or more of the techniques in this book to improve the bottom line of your freelance business? Send an email to Jake@BoomvangCreative.com with your story!

 Quick Tip: Ask Dr. Freelance

Do you have a question about pricing, estimating or any other freelance topic? Send an email to advice@DearDrFreelance.com.

Acknowledgments

Each of us is the sum of our experiences, and I am so fortunate to have enjoyed the company and guidance of some incredible folks over the years. My sincere thanks and appreciation to:

Jane Gerke, my graphic designer, who presents me with so many fantastic ideas that it's always difficult to choose. In addition to unfailingly making projects shine for clients on partnered projects, she was incredibly patient and downright unflappable during the publishing process of this book. Jane, you rock! RubiStudioDesign.com

Bonnie Mills, my editor/proofreader, who not only can spot an incorrectly italicized comma at 50 paces but also managed to find the title of this book buried in the text—which didn't surprise me at all. Bonnie, your unblinking honesty and editorial wisdom are a powerful combination. SentenceSleuth.blogspot.com

The many freelance colleagues, business clients and editors who have served as mentors and confidants over the years, and whose insights were essential to harvesting the contents of this book: Eileen, Bob, Sally, Cathy, Gary, Chip, Suzanne, Dave, Valerie, Noelle, Jim, Cyndi, Michelle, Barbara, Jenn, Corky, Steve, Laurie, Kim, Lori, Nancy, Patti, Laurie, Ken, Fripp, Debbie, Fred and so many others that I could fill another chapter just listing them all.

The professors who shepherded me along the writing and editing path, and the coaches who helped me tap into mental toughness that I never would have found on my own: Tom McGraw, Sara Suleri Goodyear, George Fayen, Dave Vogel and Ed Quattlebaum.

Finally, my family, whose creative input, support and never-ending questions took me to a whole 'nother level. Thanks for indulging me on those nights when I needed to sneak back into the office to write just one more paragraph. I'm a lucky guy.

Appendix I – Sample Estimate

ESTIMATE   **Estimate:** #00000
                                                                   Date: Month 00, 20XX

 YOUR LOGO   1234 Sunnyside Drive   **Customer:**
Would Go in this Space   Anytown, NY 08012   Client Name/Title
                          Phone/Fax/Email   Client Company Name
                          www.WebsiteAddress.com   1001 Easy Street, Suite 409
                                                     Anytown, NY 08012

PROJECT DESCRIPTION:

Editorial services for COMPANY PROJECT NAME

SCOPE OF WORK:

Services:
• Participating in Team Proposal Review on MONTH DAY X via teleconference

• Performing an editorial review of previous COMPANY materials

• Making preliminary recommendations on content/organization/approach

• Working with COMPANY production team on editing of Word document
 • Unifying overall "voice" to create concise, grammatically correct content
 • Improving organization, in particular removing redundant content
 • Focusing marketing angle

• Creating original content, approximately XXX words

• Doing research/attending meetings /corresponding as needed

• Doing three rounds of revisions

Billing: Estimated range: $X,XXX to $X,XXX. Final invoice to reflect actual time/materials.
Work outside the scope of this estimate will be billed at $XXX/hr.

Timeline: Project to commence upon receipt of XX% deposit and signed Agreement;
projected completion of edited first draft 5 business days later.

Thank you for giving me the opportunity to work with you on this project.
Please contact me at XXX-XXX-XXXX if you need me to clarify any of the proposed services.

Sincerely,

[SIGNATURE]

---

*DISCLAIMER: *This represents a simple, generic document for discussion purposes only and may not be suitable for all projects, clients or circumstances. I highly recommend you consult with an attorney or other legal expert.*